To Pastor Carol and David

From: Dan and June
Wiese

Christmas 1992

Cry of Understanding

Poems of
William Andrew Graham

VANTAGE PRESS
New York / Los Angeles

FIRST EDITION

Published by Vantage Press, Inc.
516 West 34th Street, New York, New York 10001

Manufactured in the United States of America
ISBN: 0-533-08588-8

Library of Congress Catalog Card No.: 89-90214

In Memory of Opal Bernice Graham

There's a light shining in the depth of my soul
Allowing your love to linger far into its afterglow,
Causing rays of light and tears to fall,
Sharing our rainbow to one and all.
Letting them know all love is to pass on,
Where many shall have a chance to sing her song.
Like the light shining in the depth of my soul
It's reaching out to touch me and tell me so.
That I had been chosen, yet who else could be?
Knowing our love was forever through all eternity.

Contents

Foreword

May the poems within,
Start a glow again.
To grow and shine
Till the end of time.
By letting us know,
Now and then.
Our whole purpose in life
Is to live like Him.

Acknowledgment

Cry of understanding is the one thing
I believe most are looking for in this world.
That's why we cry out in so many ways,
Some write poems, others paint, still others
Have chosen to build tall buildings to leave their mark,
Saying, "Here I am. I too need a cry of understanding."

Wildwoods

Down through the fields of sweet clover,
That's where I am longing to be.
In the dear old wildwoods
Where my love and I used to see
Bluebirds nesting in trees of oak and pine.
In fresh streams flowing, fish of all kind

Down in the dear old wildwoods
Are days I am longing for.
When our youth kept us walking
And wondering afar.

Yes, those days are gone.
Now only memories remain
Of the dear old wildwoods
That will forever seen tame.

For we have grown and drifted apart,
Yet those memories we shared
In the wildwoods
Will always be in our heart.

Face of Simone

A face that shows you Ireland,
Whether it be Killarney or Kildare.
Her skin so fresh and lovely,
Truly, a sweetness beyond compare.

She took my heart in one moment,
As I saw her standing there,
Near the Castle of Dromoland,
At its lake ever so clear.

The trees show a rare beauty,
Yet her laughter makes them seem only fair.
For she's a rose among the living,
That shall set all eyes to stare.

I am so glad I went to Ireland.
For even if my eyes become dark
Like uncut stone,
I would still have this vision
Of a little Irish cailin girl, Simone.

A Moment in Spring

Sometimes when the winter is over
And the snow disappears,
I look for that moment in spring
When flowers start to appear.
Where I may look at life,
Knowing Mother Nature is still the same,
That I am still the same old guy
Yet slowly have made a change.

Accepting these gifts from God,
Believing they will always be the same.
So that I may go forth
To sustain the life I was chosen to gain.
Through loving faith and trust in my fellow man,
When God's grace is shown.
We shall all live and learn to understand.

Never Alone

When getting old and life's troubles you fear,
Ask from God who thinks of you so very dear.
He loves and cares for each of us
In a very special way.
Even when you think you have been lost that day,
Just ask His help and He'll always see you through,
No matter what you might do.

All people in this world need help, you see,
And I know that means you and me.
So never give up when day is done,
Just think of life and what we have won.

For living each day and being able to pray
Is worth more than all the gold, they say.
What is life worth without a good night's rest
That only comes to those God has blessed?

So quit worrying about those troubles you fear,
And remember that God is always near.
Just ask and He will comfort you,
Letting you live each day anew.

Love for a Moment

I found love for a moment in a face that was true.
My eyes were entangled within a sea of blue,
Knowing at first glance I was in love with you.

Your smile told me as I looked your way.
You loved me too if it was only for this day.
I looked your body over in a second or two.
The loveliness of your golden hair and freshness of your
    skin
Just starting my genes aching, as a lover, but not in sin.

It was love for a moment as we took a chance to stare.
Only a few seconds yet we knew to truly care.
So even love that lasts only a moment
Can sometimes be true though rare.

So dream of me now and then, as I share a thought of you.
Time may come when we could meet again,
If not, I will not remain too unhappy or blue,
For I shall always remember the sparkle in your eyes
And the love that kept shining through.

Someday

I, too, may someday shine as a star,
Out in the heavens where You are.
In the milky way of Your domain,
I hope the lights within remain.
Let the work on earth I ever do
Be the many truths from only You,
Just longing to be a son stands
For wonders yet to come.

For of man only the love of Christ
Was truly shown.
He leads alone in the path of life
For us to believe and walk not in strife.
All things we gain in faith alone
Must come from things never shown.
Like the love of one's neighbor
And the forgiving of sin
That all of us are living in.

We must keep faith in God above
And forever live in His true love.
Sharing together all wonders undone,
Then maybe someday we could become a son.
For that's the real reason for man on earth:
To share light and love toward the Lord,
The One who truly allows birth.

Never Give Up

What makes you think I'll disagree
Just because your way of life is indifferent to me?
We can be friends even though we drift apart,
For there had to be something there before
Our relationship was ever to start.
The way we think or sometime see
Is all it takes for that certain feeling to be.

Two people together now and then,
And before you know it, you have a new friend.
Just by saying some chosen words they care to hear,
You'll find that this person may be ever so dear.

So never give up in thoughts of others;
They may need some one to lean on.
Not everyone is strong and a leader among men,
Most are to be followers, looking for the light to guide them.
What better hope for any man than to help show the way
For those who seem not to understand?

Man

Have you ever looked at that fellow over there,
The one who's skin is lighter or darker than yours
And has a different hair?
Would you believe he's your brother
And had the same father and mother?

I am talking now of a time in the past,
When this old world started for man.
How it multiplied ever so fast.
Eve had the genes, they say, to cause
All races to be.
So they could multiply to cover the earth
For God to see.

There's a great lesson for all to learn
Why man is of so much concern.
For with sin in everyday life
It's not hard to understand why we live in strife.

For the lust of life and the hate we form
Is really where we find most of our harm.
If we would read the scriptures,
And truly believe the words of God above,
We might be thankful
To live for ever in His true love.

If

If you have a chance to live your life again,
Would you do the same things over
And just live in sin?
Or would you try and be a light for all people to see,
Sharing your love truly with your family,
Letting each person grow in the closeness they share,
Really living as a man and wife should?
This time I would truly share the many
Thoughts and feelings of fatherhood.

I would even take the time to smile and grin,
Always share my true thoughts within.
Since I've lost her, I know the price we must pay.
And that's the reason I would be different in every way.
If our lives we could relive again,
The spring of eternal hope we might share at last,
And this would surely erase some of the problems of the
      past.

Life Anew

Your wedding day has came at last,
It's finding some future in releasing the past.
Making life happy with new thoughts in mind,
Of what tomorrow may bring, a joy in time.
For most are given one day somehow due,
When sharing love's moments with that someone new.

Things may seem different at least to a few,
Yet, just think, you're starting together anew.
Not someone living in moments of sin?
Believing God has chosen of you to remember Him,
When sharing a marriage by laws made right.
Giving true joy toward motherhood,
Because of judgement written long ago in life's twilight.

So trust in your faith with God in prayer,
Believing He never forgets and is always there
To share in all troubles you may find night or day,
Allowing some rest and peace when you choose to pray,
Knowing He is your father and mother, too.
From given spirit within,
A knowledge in life of unknown test due,
For His love shall ever remain in life anew.

Contentment

Where is this place called contentment?
Oh, where, oh, where can it be.
Believing in the future and the more I read
Of all the beauty about that's here to see,
Just what more should you need?

Have you not taken the time to look about
At all the wonders we have to share
In things yet to come
Of which there will be none to compare?

For the streets will be paved with gold,
With jewels of every kind,
But the greatest gift of all
Will be the love within that shall always shine.

There need not be the moon or stars above,
For our light will be from this every-giving love.
Knowing God will be with us every day,
Because it has been through His light that we found the
    way.

Family of Man

Every day I ask myself,
What is there in life I hope to achieve?
When I speak of Him I am at perfect rest,
For each day I find life is but some test.
Wherein things of truth and love we do care,
And are in most of us to share.

For in loving others we make all things plain.
Like the name of someone dear to us,
In them there is never any shame.
With these thoughts I have kept in mind
Are the truths I believe in and often find.

I really believe in my poems I have found art,
Where about Him I shall never forget or part.
For I have found my way through love to understand
And truly respect the family of man.

Somewhere in Time

In time to come He will call them and they must part.
No longer will they share that chosen start.
This is a true test in life that has just begun,
For they must ask of Him to share
The load in life that is truly undone.

It won't be easy to live without her in life,
That loving partner you shared as your wife.
You will find some days were tests unfold,
Where you ask of Him to come take your very soul.

Yet if you shared the things of truth in His light,
He will comfort you by seeing you through.
For you are His child to be, through love, you will see.
What is there in life after death,
If not to come to the Lord's house for rest?

And later still to climb upon some chosen hill
That our Lord only can instill,
Where in everyday life there will be no more pain,
For in the book of life He chose to find your name.

Desire

Don't count the miles between us;
They don't matter much at all.
Just count the many joys we've shared,
The big ones and the small.

Count the thoughts that bring us closer,
The memories we found so dear.
Then the miles that lie between us
Will just seem to disappear.

So count the many blessings
We shared along life's road.
In knowing it's how you live your life,
And of where you hoped to go.

The Letter

I write this letter because it may be my final hope.
I've asked what is there for me?
What must I do to cope or have an audience with You?
I've read my whole life about saints and of chosen
    fishermen
Who have been true. I, too, am a fisherman yet time is
    long overdue
Where in life I, too, hope to find an answer to what I must
    do.

To have a chance to speak to You and find some answer
    of what to do,
In making my life worth living or dying, whatever my case
    will be.
I have suffered much in life and felt real pain,
Not knowing or finding wherein I could have a reason
To follow Your way.

Although each day I see all the wonderment
That scripture tells if we could only keep the faith.
Yet I feel like others from the past;
I may see some wonderful valley, yet never reach the
    promised land.

I guess from time long gone You have already judged some
    or most
And have already chosen Your plan.
So what must I do if I am ever to find my way
Where I, too, could be a son, and understand.

Intriguing Lady

If I open my heart and let you inside,
Would it hurt the one you love,
Or give you a feeling to hide?

You seem so happy,
Yet I feel there's a truth only you can show.
Even as a stranger, I feel I seem to know.

This is such a terrible shame,
For I can see by all who love you,
Your mountains are rich with gold.

Life seems full, yet I guess as the out one
I may even know there's oh,
So many needs in life you have yet to sow.

So if ever I may help you, maybe only in prayer,
I hope you find your true place in life
Forever to share with that someone who will always care.

Caring for Others

Like buds on trees in the spring of the year,
Life starts over again.
When you wake in the morning
And the sunshine brightens your day,
Let yourself go; be the most you can in every way.

Throw your love toward all directions,
And like the wind,
It shall go about to help all people within.
If you let others know you really care,
They will help make your day and with you
They will share.

When you see a friend or others feeling low,
Smile and try to help them make it through that day.
Treat them with all the love within,
Showing you care for each in a special way.

Just be thankful everyday, letting others know you care.
About a better place in which to live,
Also by showing loving thoughts of others,
You will also receive much more than you give.

In Search of Thee

What will I do, how must I find the way of truth and light?
Will I ever be forgiven of past sins
That have haunted me both day and night?
How many mountains must I climb
Before I find where the light will always shine?

In searching so long now, wondering if I might go astray,
I find when keeping my faith each day as I pray,
It's starting to grow stronger, this feeling that
Almost got away.
When finding some peace I hope it will be as a song
That shall comfort or instill in me
All the truth I believe has came along.

I have never given up in hope of what's to be.
With love of truth a light will always shine in me.
Always keeping this faith, believing in One
That in some way I will be part of His vine,
Which will allow me to become a son.

Cry of Understanding

Often we, the lucky ones, never stop and wonder why
Keith and Joe are such troublemakers; and or why they
seem to be so mean. Too often of these lives little is
known and so very much never seen.
Most of these young fellows and girls come from broken
homes where the mother or father don't even get
along. They're always fighting, showing most of their
hate or lust within?
They have forgotten the wonders they could have had
when being humble with each other, trying to
overcome troubles they do not wish to understand.

Yes, it is always easy to see other peoples faults; not our
own, but most of us come from loving families. We do
not really understand the way these kids feel.
They have no one to love or try to understand that when
tomorrow comes, what's going to happen to them?
Most think there is no God.
For where has He been in their lives? This is the reason
these kids gather together. They feel no one cares
about them. For if God is to help all who cry out, they
ask, and I am sure most have, oh God, where are You?
For they are as human as you and I. Most people in life
get lost somewhere along the way; that's what's wrong
with these kids' parents.

Some of these poor souls get a few joints of some kind of
weed; they smoke them to get away from it all to that
land of fantasy. Yet when their so-called trip is over
they still must come back to everyday life where all
things are still the same. The same problems are there
and will always be there until they make up their minds

to accept the fact that they are humans who need help through understanding.

If they're lucky enough, God will call them. Maybe some will open their minds to Scripture, the Bible, and they will see that in all of life's trouble, He will find them a way.

For all through life the history of things are pretty much the same.

When the family has broken down everything seems to fall apart. Without leadership nothing seems to go right. Even a ship has a captain to be the leader to see to it that all things are working perfectly, each person doing his or her job to complete the mission, no matter what.

So one can pretty well say that the father in the home should be the leader and teacher of what is best for the family, and through love and proper discipline, to teach the ways of truth and happiness. It's very sad when men cannot lead their family toward truth or understanding of all problems.

He and his mate just do not want the responsibility of taking care of anyone.

Yet only through work, when people give of each toward better things will people ever hope to cope with everyday life.

Nothing worth having comes easy to most people; we have to really work hard most of the time. But if we ask God to help in all things of everyday life, and try doing what is right by the law of truth and light, which are in Scripture for all who care to read, then we will find some peace and contentment in this life.

All I Need

Will I ever finish this poem for Opal?
The one who was ever true?
Who always thought of others, like me and you?
I have been writing for so long and yet
I just can't seem to find the words to say
How much I think of her each and every day.

I thought that by now, since nine years have passed,
That I would have found a way at last.
Even though I hope and pray for some release,
I know within the depth of my heart,
My loving memories of her will never part.

For I have been one of the lucky ones
Who had really found the way of truth
And peace in each day's morning sun.
Having had such love to share each and every day,
I cry every now and then when thinking
Of all the joy we knew.
What more can life give than true love
That has made each day life anew?

A Friend

Here as I write and try to say
Some words helpful toward each every day,
Knowing most of us have so much to tell.
If we would put the words together that often spell
How we really feel about one another,
Yet cannot say "I love you" as a brother.

We feel this is taking something away from a man.
But have you ever said to some friend, "I love you,
I really love you" and will try to understand?
When you say these kind words that are from the heart,
Notice the glowing happiness in your friend's eyes,
And maybe a tear or two as he leaves to depart.

Knowing there could be no greater joy
Than the feeling of one's self
When they take the time to care or try to understand.
For in doing so it shall make him so much more a man.
This special gift in life we all hope to receive,
Stands no farther away than you and me.

Neighborhood Bar

Oftentimes when sitting at the neighborhood bar,
Drinking a glass of beer,
I cannot help but watch as people come and go,
Wondering just what may be the many troubles they fear.
Some losing jobs, not having money to pay the bills?
Or having had a fight with the wife,
Because they were both getting older
And life between each had lost some of its thrills.

We all seem to go through these problems and strife,
For this is all part of the game of living:
Trying to overcome the many changes of life
That will never stay the same.
Yet maybe if we took the time to try again,
Most of the problems would be as the wind,
Just coming and going now and then?

The important thing in life, I see,
Are children and friends that make up family.
So try with all your heart and mind
To find the things in life you lost along the line.
Try being man and wife again, starting each day in prayer
You will both live again if you share
With one another in this chosen light
Which will help you make it both day and night.

A Wish

If I had one wish and it was truly for me,
I know what's in my mind if only my heart would agree
Of these mixed emotions for what I have chosen, or hope
    to be.
I have been reading the Bible most of my life,
Believing in all thoughts of written scripture I see.

It is said that the fear of God is the start of wisdom
That all men should hope to achieve.
For when they have been called by our Lord,
These minds will be opened to receive
Where most of their earthly problems will be helped,
If not relieved.

So if I got my one wish and that might well be,
To follow my master's way
Where truth and love will set me free.

A Story Told

Have you ever looked over toward the other side of the hill,
And wonder why the grass seems greener still.
Or why some days the sky is bluer in contrast,
Where in ways it seems so peaceful allowing rest at last?
Understanding all these wonders are here for us to share,
That is what scripture has to say for those who truly care.

Someday in time yet to be, the Lord will show us a given way,
That is, to those of us who could never see or choose to pray.
A new door shall be opened where all will take notice
Of His everlasting love and greatness yet to be.
For most did not read of His words, of if they did
They just would not let their minds believe?

For He spoke in parables which all men should hope to
    solve,
In doing so their minds will be opened to wonders allowed.
Like the joy that must come not of moon or stars above,
But of the true love that will be shared from everyone.

Railroad Man

We all belong to the family of man; for me this is the
    railroad clan.
It is a way of life I have chosen to know,
When switching cars in different yards wherever I am apt
    to go.
To most people I show we are much alike in one way or
    the other,
When you stop and think, the other fellow is your brother.

Even our lives are pretty much the same; we all have wants,
That have us go to work each day to make up or switch a
    train.
What we do is that of sharing in life, needed hours,
Helping each other in some way undoing excess strain.
My job was the foreman of a train called the heavy hauler,
Going everywhere, hauling all kinds of freight
And a lot of happiness to spare.

Knowing this railroad job is a way of life,
When showing kindness toward most you find joy, not
    strife.
I have been at this job so long now things would seem
    strange,
If I would be forced to quit or make a sudden change.
Like I said before and I may say again,
Most people I work with are more like brothers than
    friends.
Being one big happy family of man, working together,
    hopefully
To understand.

Thoughts

Sometimes when you think you have lost the way,
You have forgotten the closeness of children at play,
Or the singing of a song; even the birds and the sky above,
Are here to share in all moments of love.
For the Lord moves in such a wonderful way,
Allowing happiness to be found in each life every day.

Just being together a short time on this beautiful earth,
You must truly be thankful of all its charm and worth.
So when you think you have had it rough from undue pain,
You have just forgotten the many blessings you have
      gained.
Yet if you pray to God for the things you really need,
You'll find that He will always send a special seed.

Yes, the many truths you thought you had lost
Will come into mind again,
Making you remember they were there all the time,
Just like the coming and going of His wind.

I Care

Whenever you are sad and lonely or have moments of
    dismay,
Remember there is always someone who thinks of you
Whenever he chooses to pray
Who never is tired or weary, for you're only a thought away.
Believe me, as I still think of you each and every day.

It seems only yesterday when a little girl with dolls
Used to play.
Now you are all grown, leaving the dolls on display.
Yet if days again seem dreary, unkind, or sad,
There is someone to always help—just think of Dad.

He's been down life's road and around much longer than
    you.
It's just taken this Dad longer to express
Feelings of love long overdue.
Yet never doubt of what he might do,
For he has always loved you as his daughter
And will his whole life through.

Garden of Eden

My garden of Eden is no further than the faith I have in
    God!
For in His loving grace we share in a moment of rest.
Yes the wonderment of the mind that can seeming flow,
When open to understanding that true love allows to grow.
Where in trust to let you live as His child to be,
Believing as part of this vine you are forever free.

From all the entangled hurt of life in strife,
Knowing of truth from light and faith in Thee,
We may find this garden in which we all hope to be:
Where all of life can be as it should,
Sharing true love among all people in brotherhood.

A Man's Share

Lord, will I ever find that place of contentment
Where I might have peace of mind?
I believe and feel I am not too far away,
Yet I cannot seem to pace myself in proper time.
Even knowing my love for You is strong,
Down in my heart somehow I know as scripture will say,
It takes more than just love or thoughts I have when I pray.
Man must help his brother and with him share,
The wants of life that weigh us all,
Even though some seem more blessed of Your call.

So when someone asks for help and they rely on you.
Think of all the good your apt to do.
If you find a way within yourself to help that one in need,
Look for others that might care to give of their seed.
For man does not live alone, he has that choice to help
        others,
That just can't seem to make it on their own.
So with all the love of your heart,
Give the best of yourself, and please let it be known!

The Flag

I look at Old Glory waving at half mast,
Remembering our country and its enjoyable past.
Knowing I am like many from this great land,
Hoping to grow through love where I might understand.
I took a trip that comes to each and everyone,
Whether they are in judgment or not they still must come.
For we laid my Father to rest while the minister would share
Moments among us in prayer, thanking all for being there,
Letting us know this would not be his final call,
For in time we shall all gather in God's great Kingdom hall.

Somewhere along the way I had forgotten what Old Red
    White
And Blue had meant to folks like me and you,
So now I take more pride in the way I look at this flag
With feelings that are intently new.
Knowing it helps me remember things worth fighting for,
Like our Liberty and the right to speak of one's God and
    Lord.

Allowing all to enjoy the wonders of this great land,
Yet most of all their rights through freedom to understand.
So if you are somewhat like me and forget what you really
    have
In this great land of ours, stop and look at Old Glory at
    half mast
In some national cemetery and think of all the men and
    women
Who have fought and cared to share in the many rights
    in finding
Peaceful rest at last.

A Plan for Man

Have you ever thought of the loneliest depth in space
Or why man was created? and upon the earth placed
Of all the planets from this great universe we see,
Have you ever wondered why earth was chosen for you
    and me?
I believe in time it will be proven as scripture must say,
The Lord wanted a testing place for all to come and stay.

And this earth happens to be that place to grow by planted
    seed
Where we shall some day engulf all the universe of space
    with Thee.
I somehow think this is the master plan
For all of us who belong to the family of man.
So never give up or lose faith in Him,
For when the time comes we shall all live again,
Sharing in God's glory for what He had planned for man.

My Call

All people have a calling in life.
We, the lucky ones, find out which way to go.
I have been favored when being called by You
To write the words that often tell a few
Chosen thoughts, helping some, no matter who.
It has taken these long years of pain and
Suffering to allow me to know

That my call has been to write poetry
For all of the world to see
Of the many truths in family life and love
In all Scripture they may choose to read.
For I believe I am just another tool,
Being used in such a wonderful way.

What more can any man ask of Thee
Than to help some lost soul find that seed?
Believing what else but joy after death
Can he ever hope to find,
Where we shall be risen to become a part of
Your living vine.

The Light at Road's End

While traveling down life's road, this load I am carrying
I can no longer bear.
I have been told there is a pleasant valley somewhere,
And a lovely garden in which I might share.
Where there's plenty of food and rest beyond compare.
I hope with all my being, I find this place today,
For I am growing tired and the light at the end of the road
Every once in a while fades away.

It really scares me to think for some strange reason
To feel I can no longer run the course in life I felt
I was always to do.
For in searching I hoped someday to find You
To instill within me the strength to keep looking
And always find light at the end of each day's run,
In doing so I would believe within myself that I
Could also some day be Your son.

A Rest

What is the price we must pay
To live out our lives each and every day?
For high are mountains we might climb
To ensure some peace within our mind
When fleeing from troubles we care not to face
Because of dough or undue disgrace.

Even though at times they seem small,
Yet they are ever so hard to pay.
I find that when I am at road's end,
Life for me must truly just begin.
For I ask of Him, my Lord and God, through prayer,
To help me find that place where He and I
Would together always care to share
All the peaceful rest at His command,
Believing then and only will I truly understand.

Why Me, Lord?

What is this feeling I hold within my mind,
That has me speak and write poems of You all the time?
At times I feel as though my mind is gone, as if mad.
Yet when Your closeness comes I am very happy.
Glad that I have been chosen to write poems
Others may read, knowing this is nothing new,
Just another time in life where others are
Listening or reaching out toward You,
Hoping You might guide them in this way of flight,
Where they, too, will find words of meaning in life

To help erase some of the strife most are living in.
For the Bible says that toward the end Satan will do
    anything
To try and overcome or even win.
So let us keep on writing for those seeking faith anew,
To dine on Your love, with uplifting thoughts about You,
Knowing that when You call,
They have been helped by one of the greatest gifts of all:
The spirit that allows them to make this run,
Where with truth and love they may become a son.

A Choice

Oftentimes when I am about to pray,
I cannot seem to make up my mind about what I should say,
Thinking only of what I might do to become a son.
Though in thoughts of others I hope they may find,
From the words I put together some help in time.
That is, if they choose to read, and I hope most will,
Allowing me some sort of joy from undue skill.

For these words I am sure God must choose uplifting me,
Knowing of their enlightenment for all who may read.
By letting us know of love in which we must be concerned,
With study of the scripture and trying to learn.
For these gifted words are of life itself,
Never to be misread or just left on some distant shelf.

His words are the very essence of man's soul,
Always showing the way one step at a time.
All that is ever asked is that we come to His table to dine
On all the truths within, sharing help in this world of sin.
When opening this book of life, allow yourself to find that
It is love through kindness that brings peace of mind.

Now and Then

Our way of life started long ago when God created man,
Hoping he might grow.
Yet as Scripture will say, man slowly drifted away
To follow the ways of Satan by whom he was swayed.
Adam listened to his mate whom he loved and believed.
Eve loved Adam and never thought of him to deceive.
Yet Eve listened to Satan, who lied, not just then, but
Even in this day and will till the very end.
So remember this is a lesson of much concern
For all of us who care for faith and try to learn

When you long for life and all the truth within,
Open your heart when letting God in.
Knowing if man had faith as God above,
He would not be lustful, hateful, but live as the dove.
Where he might have peace of mind, letting love
Be a way of life.
Then he would find, living God's way above all,
A chosen place to find rest until His call.

Forever Love

Often at night when stars are bright
And the moon is light above,
I think of times long ago
When our hearts were full of love.
Always looking to be together, never
Dreaming about the time we may have to part.

But in spring of the year
When the leaves are always with morning dew
My heart told me that you already knew
That it was just a matter of time
When you would no longer be mine.
For our life on earth was to be
Never again for you and me.

I knew, my dear, you had been taken away.
Now only in memories shall I find some way
To help me make it through each unkind day.
Your suffering on earth will no longer be.
Allowing a special blessing for you and me,
Knowing our love is in hope of joy to come
With that life forever through eternity.

Again

If I had my life to live over again
I would be open and more thoughtful of others,
More loving, and try to become more like Him,
The one who lets all become a son.
When sharing the cares of fatherhood,
Of giving the wonders undone.

I would share more of the loves in life,
Toward really caring about children and wife.
Trying to shine like the morning sun,
Allowing all doubts of love to have been won.
Making the most of each spoken word, knowing
Each voice would always be heard.
Having those who love and try,
Know I would always help till the day I die.

So if I had my life to live again
I would be someone you could always trust,
Like our Lord, the Potter, who formed us,
Then added the living soul,
The most important part, His special gift within.
So now you know why I would like to live like Him,
If I could but live my life again.

Where Am I?

I live in a house now quite alone,
Where once cries of laughter were often known.
The children used to run and play;
Having happy smiles on their faces made my day.
I had all these joys that came from life, at least
Of loving one's family and living in peace.
Day after day with loving prayer,
I asked for guidance of my life to share
So some of the hate within might cease.
Knowing in many ways life can seem cruel;
This often happens when we forsake the golden rule.

Yet to know again of happy times back then,
That surely come when a little child may smile or grin.
By praying and seeking God's way I found joy the other
     day.
Together again at Christmastime,
Once more with loving family I chose to dine.
Where am I now seems like I truly know,
For it is love of family that allows a child to grow.
And I am a child of God in so many ways now shown,
Hoping to become an adult
To teach from the light within all true thoughts known.

Longing

Help me, God, O Lord, I pray, that I may find a way.
Let me know which way to go
To find some needed peace to help my soul.
Please let me feel Your gentle hand
And let them know and understand.

The road's been rough these many years,
Filled with pain and filled with tears.
Please let me know what I am to say
To help them all day by day.

I love them all and want to please,
But someone is always hurt by me.
I lean toward one regret or the other,
I'm not a wife, I'm not a mother.
Yet someday they will discover,
That about them I care and share
All my loving thoughts in prayer.

Opal's Garden

My garden will have many roses
And other kinds of flowers,
A place where I may hide away
To dream of chosen hours.
Some place that is quiet and peaceful
To truly be alone,
A little spot among the flowers
Somehow my very own.

Someday I'll take along someone
I hold so true and dear
To share my peace and happiness,
Banishing all their doubts or fear.
I hope someday to have this place
For it means so much to me,
But if I don't I'll be content
Through thoughts of love in memory.

Loving Parents

Is not a father still just a son born of Thee
To make life run
When sharing the joys of fatherhood
In raising a family as most should?
Just as the spreading of Your word,
The father's word should also be heard.

For all men must give of themselves
If a place in life they hope to achieve.
Where they may walk with pride and understand
What it takes to be a humble man,
Staying strong yet tender to do the job at hand.

When correcting a lonely child yet making him feel glad
He will always be loved by Mom and Dad.
For we know who else should help him grow,
Who else in life cares or loves enough to show?

No Greater Love

Opal, my love, you're so like the dove
As I sigh and think about you,
I find still as I look upon the hill
Then puts you far above me.

And someday I will truly know
Our love is to grow,
For each day seems as a year,
Making the nights all too lonely.
Soon time may call where we must part,
But Opal, my love, you will ever share my heart.

Knowing love that is true will endure,
And share shall we forever.
Believing there is one great moment
In this after life to be,
So will love always go with you and me.

Together Again

Sometimes at night when I am all alone,
I think of you, dear, and of life unknown.
There is a place in time where we shall meet,
Being ever so humble and longing to seek.
As on earth today and in time to come,
It's true love that comes for some.

Like spreading the word of our Lord;
The many truths of His love's reward.
Where if we really love and let Him share,
The darkness about will not flare,
Allowing His true light always to be shown
To those of us that have somehow known.

There is a great space in God's domain
Of all the things to come yet are still the same.
For it is the call of God above,
Which really instills the true meaning of love.
So now you know, for now and then,
With God's own love we shall be together again.

Blessed Lord

Blessed Lord, I believe I have found my way.
Your grace has shown all around me that is this day.
As I woke up this morning I gave thanks in prayer.
Of this some times we are short and with You, unfair.
Although I truly don't know what life would be without you,
You seem to walk with me each and every day.
I am so thankful for Your love and kindness and watching
    You do,
Even when there are times I forget to pray.

I feel so terribly sorry for all misguided souls
Who think there is no God in heaven,
Believing it is only wishful thinking of these or those.
Yet You and I know better, for we're only a seed apart.
You are my heavenly Father; I am a son of art
So I place my hands with Thine until the proper time,
When some shall be called to share of Your living vine.

Mother Mine

Mother mine, I'll find some way
To take you home again
Across the wild and rambling sea
To you dear old Ireland.
We'll find that space to make a home,
Staying forever, never again to roam.
You gave me life of a special kind
That allows oh, such love to ever shine
Between a mother and her child
To last more than some given moment
From an oncoming smile,
Showing, all the earth of love that's won
When it's shared between a mother and her son.

What more could any son hope to do
Than to see her happy through and through.
The One who chose to give him birth
Never any doubts of his love are worth,
For he did return his mother mine
To dear old Ireland again to find
Some peace on earth till the very end,
Allowing Her choice sod knowing she
Was truly happy again.

And he also left a place beside her soul,
Believing in time this where he would go.
After sharing a life together over there,
Where else would a son care to be
Other than this choice sod truly beyond compare,
Saying; "Mother mine, I showed the way
Allowing us both to be home again
After crossing the wild and rambling sea
To our future home in dear old Ireland."

Farewell, My Friend

While most people in this life just seem to come and go,
My thoughts of you shall always grow.
Because each day of work you seemed to greet me
With a morning smile when telling me hello.
I know to some it may be just a word,
Yet I know from being around you
It's meant as it should be when heard.

You are using your way of planting a morning seed
To help start others on their way,
With a smile and a kind thought for that day.
To me you will always be remembered as one
Who took the time when saying, "Hello, have a nice day,"
And of happiness I hope you find.

I don't think I need say anything more or add to my view,
For it has been my pleasure working and being around you.
So farewell, my friend, till we cross that space in time,
Where we shall be together as part of God's everlasting vine.

The Tree at Dromoland Castle

There is a tree at Dromoland Castle near a lake so clear.
I love to stand near her for she is a gift of God so dear.
And when you look at all the beauty she has to possess
You might understand why I fell in love, more or less.
She is like a giant among most; her limbs so large and
    strong,
Giving shades of green so colorful as nature's song.

The floor mat of her trunk is a field of evergreen.
So make this trip to Dromoland Castle to see what I mean.
For when you see this tree so sturdy and bold,
You will know where I found my pot of gold.

The picture she gives you of love and strength galore
Will live in your memory ever more.
Like the planting of the Lord's seed, a tree is free
So with love in my heart I say to you,
'Tis Dromoland Castle you must go and pursue.

Lady Sheila

The land ship of Ireland, *Lady Sheila* be her name.
She took us from the town of Shannon to the port of
     Galway Bay.
Jim Kelly was her skipper and a fine one he be.
He would scurry every port for all to see.
He knows all the important places about the land and sea.
His history of Ireland is well versed and true,
Making the trip understanding for strangers as me and you.
Shirley Dooley was the first mate, and a lovely one at that.
She, too, knows a lot about the history of Ireland,
And believe me, she sure loves to chitchat.

The passengers that made this journey in the year of
     eighty-five,
Will forever be in memory, be they dead or alive.
I found in our togetherness,
A treasured moment in life that shall always be in access.
Leaving, one finds a safe harbor in his mind forever,
While we sailed the highway and byways near the heather,
Allowing us to savor the greens and golds of Ireland
In the fields around Dublin Bay.

So if you're thinking of traveling that land across the sea,
Find the land ship *Lady Sheila*.
Her captain, Jim Kelly, will be more than happy to make
     your day.
To sail along the highway over mountains near the bay,
Truly showing you Ireland as it need be.
Once more I would like to say: If you take a trip to Ireland
And happiness is your order for the day,
Hop aboard the *Lady Sheila*, go with Jim and Shirley all
     the way.

Thoughts of You

When dreaming of you dear, every now and then,
Wondering just how long it has been
Since I held you in my arms and felt your warm caress,
Knowing never again will I feel this happiness.

Where most of my days are usually blue,
This happens when I am not thinking of you,
For these thoughts of you are all I have
To see me through.
Though I thought by now, after all this time,
I would have been able to adjust my mind.

But when love has been strong, you never forget.
Somehow you know that you're not over it yet.
A need is still there, an ache beyond compare
Of sweet loving memories we once had to share.

Yet I will never complain of the many thoughts of the past,
Just ever be thankful that they will always last,
Allowing me to now and then dream of you,
Sharing some peace of mind in things I do.

Morning Birds

Where are the morning birds that used to sing aloud,
When dancing on my window sill,
Playing among their own exciting crowd.
I sure miss the noise and flutter of wing,
Of feet dancing to some song as they chose to sing
While they fluttered about on the gutterspout.

My day seems lonely without God's toys
That start me thinking of the wonder of life and its joys.
To me the birds are like some children playing a game;
There is so much excitement in the joys they claim.
Letting me know no day could be complete
Till I hear some bird sing his enlightening song,
Then I might appear quite as myself the rest of the day on.

Sometimes I look at trees and wonder if birds are there,
The sky seems still, never a slant of life to share.
Then without a whisper, like some magical surprise,
A little bird appeared; he just flew before my eye.
So now I believe I can start my day,
For the Lord has shown another creation in life today.
The bird's of joy never truly went away,
They had just flown to another tree to rest or play.

Picture on the Wall

I have a picture on the living room wall
That tells the story of it all.
A smile that is true and eyes that shine,
These help me think of another time,
When we shared together things of the past,
Like our true love we hoped would always last.

Yet every once in awhile I believe my mind is about to stray;
It starts looking for reasons to try and forget you
And go some other way. Still thoughts of you are strong,
Lingering within my mind most of the day long.

Maybe I believe different from some of the rest,
Wherein thinking my love will always be of excess.
With that feeling of never being completely alone,
By us living our lives, believing true love would never stray,
That we will forever share this light
That has always shown the way.

Spanish Lake

At the break of dawn when light first appears,
I notice the haze upon the lake,
For this is autumn, when leaves are gold and brown,
Allowing such a beautiful sight each morning we wake.
For all who may pass and choose to see
What Mother Nature has again, given you and me.
I often walk her shores every now and then
Just to find some excitement or things new around each
    chosen bend.
I remember sometime, which was really not too long ago,
I walked around her banks in the winter snow,
Taking pictures I hoped would last all of life through,
Believing in some distant time
I would not be able to walk and search her banks
Or even think of each morning when I found the dew

That formed on grasses I often chose to walk upon
While looking at Spanish Lake,
Longing of her to someday write some enticing song
To bring all neighbors from far and near
So they may share in this joy and beauty I have found so
    dear.
Just pack a basket for a day of fun in the sun or under a tree
If that is where you might choose to be.
For I was brought here as a little boy
By my father and his friend who truly showed and gave
    me a spot to forever enjoy.
Having me make this trip around Spanish Lake now and
    then,
Remembering its beauty and charm
That will forever entice me to make this trip again and
    again.

The Green Hills of Ireland

You might see the green of Ireland in some
Enchanting way,
Yet I find the hills in the country a choice
That always seems to make my day.
I have had only a few days of this blessedness sublime
And I know it's more than just some lovely dream.
For I have taken to the hills as a shepherd,
Longing only to be herding some sheep.
Remembering all the green in Ireland seems
To gather into a magical heap.

Take any hillside, look almost anywhere,
I am sure there is no place quite like it to share.
With so many different shades of green you're apt to see,
Never will there be another, such as Ireland to me.
I have asked my God in heaven to show the way I must
        roam;
He swayed me toward Ireland to find my future home,
Knowing I would love the green hills forever more,
A place to truly live and adore.

Tears

Everyone dreams of someone, no matter who they are,
My dreams are of you, dear, sometimes out too far.
Leaving nights so lonely, no room to find comfort in.
I just sit in some bar not drinking too much for I
Care to share with you,
The dreams we made together when our love was new.
I know it's been a long time since you have passed away,
Yet I ever dream of you always when I pray.
For to me you're with our Maker, each hand in hand.
Believing someday I shall join you in His promised land.

So dear, do not think too harshly of me; I cannot help
The way I feel.
Because to me you are so alive, almost real.
Yes, to me you will live forever, not only in memories.
I shall wait till my God of heaven calls me back to thee.
So until I dream tomorrow, good-night, my sweet and
　　　lovely wife.
You mean more now than ever in this sad and changing life.

Another Day

Are there no other words to come through me?
To put on paper for all the world to read?
Why have You stopped these words of charm,
That surely must help all who choose of Thy seed,
For I could never write words that would do harm.
Knowing only what I am allowed to write must be true,
And show a way of life thoughtful of You.
Believing of all love You show toward us,
Who truly love and worship in Your trust.

Please send some words again,
For they are my whole purpose in this life.
Without writing of Your way I seem to live only in strife,
Never thinking I will make it through the night.
There is nothing greater in this life for me
Than sharing words together, telling a story
For all the world to see.
I am sure You are just waiting for another day or time,
When You shall implant some choice thoughts in my mind
To tell another message to all mankind of the joy they
Could behold
When trusting You forever with body and soul.

A Pal

Life is such a wonder! No matter where you look
You will find not all things are written in a book.
There are so many things of life we have to share,
Yet so few seem to truly care.
But this friendship we have found
Will live on even if we share days that are up or down.

For it makes no difference whether we think
In terms of things large or small.
What a wonderful feeling to truly know
My mind has been opened to show and recall
The many blessings others cannot seem to see,
Like the friendship developing between you and me.

A pal is a true friend that may cause a spark to start,
At times raise all kinds of hell, even when you're down.
Yet when trouble happens he will be the first around
And the last to leave until a just truth has been found.

Space and Time

Time is endless like the many thoughts of the mind
About space and stars above clouds that roll by
And often seem to climb.
Who else but man can have this wonderment?
This strange pandemonium about objects in space.
Like rings around some planet, as men we know so little
    about,
Setting out minds to grasp of miracles
We know are to someday allow many to sing and shout.
From unseen ways we shall learn to understand
The joys of discovering the where and why of man.

For scripture does say in time to come
He will be with us of family and one mind,
To share the knowledge of outer space, of eons, of time,
And to truly know why He has chosen this for man.
The angels tried, yet many failed the test;
This should be truly of much concern
To those not keeping faith and trust in His return.
So when we are called to share in His vine,
We will see that it was worth all the pain on earth,
For those who trust and truly believe in His chosen time.

Love of Thee

Lord, why have You given me such a part in glory
That leads me along this path wherein I might find
A way of life within myself. You have chosen to let shine.
Knowing it is only from love and trust You have instilled
    in me
That I may judge with spirit when my eyes are open to see.

Believing in every drop of rain that fell from the sky above,
Should let everyone know these are the many tears of Your
    true love.
To moisten the earth for things of nature to grow,
As the spirit You send toward us of things we are to sow.

Of the light from above in truth You are to show
Having us to believe of one God allowing us to grow.
Forever caring and sharing in our many hopes of love,
Believing He, too, was a son with help from above.

Believing

As time passes by and the older I become,
I truly thank You, Lord, for making me a man.
I look with a vision of things yet to come,
Believing through prayer,
I might enchance my chance of becoming a son.
Expect of me, dear Father, things undone
Though I am ever praying I may make the run.

I have lived a fair life trying to play the game
When loving one's neighbor and believing the same.
What is said is not surprising and can be done,
Though I will wait for You to be my spiritual Father
Before I am to be Your spiritual son.
I am longing from the very depths of my soul,
Believing in time yet to come that I will truly know.

The Vine

When this earth is made over I hope to be renewed.
Believing this will only happen because of You.
You showed the way long ago
For those seeking and caring to know.
When trying Your way of life, they will understand.
That all words of scripture were written for man.
For what good could they be other than seed,
You being Lord and God of all life to be.
Yet for us they are a way of life allowing us to see,
When living by Your laws, they can set us free.

We shall always have trouble and some kind of pain,
Yet believing in Your love, we can hold on to claim
Or overcome most problems in life that cause strife.
I trust and believe all scripture I read.
For these words were written through others,
As the whole world was to see.
The Lord using many people to help show the way,
Knowing it takes more than just moving moments as we
    pray.
Man will change his whole life and start anew,
By opening his mind toward what he should truly do.
Then after this test in life has been done,
The Lord may call him to the living vine
Where he shall be loved by God as His true son.

A Seed to Plant

Flowers are a sure sign of beauty, no matter the shape or
    form.
For they are another gift sent to show of nature's charm,
In teaching a lesson of life that all should see,
While watching the growth and bloom of the planted seed.

In seeing this beauty our eyes send a message to the brain,
And we know that love thoughts should remain.
Yet the shades of flowers often change and petals fall,
Leaving seeds drop on to the earth to be enshrouded,
Knowing Mother Nature shall awaken them at her call.

Like all things that are of God's we, too, must undergo
    change.
To pass into death, be embedded somewhere in mother
    earth,
Believing in time the Lord will command a new birth.
For the Lord uses this way with all things that are of life,
Sharing only the ways of love, never the ways of strife.

Subsist

I know not why You have forsaken me.
What have I done that You should cause me so much pain?
Please, open my mind so that I may understand.
What could You expect of me? Am I some thing more than
  man?

What is my reason for living? I am so terribly sad.
There have been times I, too, have asked for rest,
To wait for the given time or Your judgement test
Of all the great and small, who are ever waiting for Your
  call,
When we shall no longer bleed from pain or undue harm,
Only joy will come to us who have lived somewhat in Your
  charm.

It has not been easy, this run of one man's life,
Living within pain and suffering this terrible strife.
Yet You tell of this the whole bible through,
If man hopes to run the test or do things to teach a few,
They may suffer and know of pain, those who care to be
  with You.
Of this I pray to God allowing me to always exist,
Being helpful in all that I can to subsist.

A Father, a Son

Why is the father so like the son?
The one who has grown in life to teach
Of things that should be done,
With a family someday he may hope to start.
By teaching of love in all things known,
When raising the children they might be shown.
There is much in life we must learn;
This comes only from us who love and are of concern.

Knowing when my son becomes a father one day,
He may have a daughter or son to seek Thy way.
Of giving themselves to others along life's road,
Longing for this special trust all should behold.
When sharing these gifts from God above
They should open their hearts and truly give of love.

Not all people could have this sight in mind,
Choosing to share their love with all mankind.
There is a cry of loneliness and despair,
When people are lost or in need of special care.
If you have that voice or the chosen words for these few,
Speak out for lost souls and try to start their life anew.

Help Me

Dear Lord, help me please; my mind is so unstable.
I fear I may cease long before I dine at Thy table.
Why oh why will You not share
All the sweet tones of love I know are there.
What have I done; I have asked forgiveness for past sins.
I start each day following You,
Yet for some unseen reason cannot seem to follow through.
Has Satan such a hold on me, that
Even praying to You will not set me free?

I have always asked each day and night in prayer
To forever let me find the comfort of You being there.
What have I done that keeps us apart?
I have truly opened my heart and mind as well,
Asking from Thy grace in which to dwell,
Where I might find some peace from within,
Knowing I will be relieved of this painful sin.
For I care not to follow the ways of Satan,
Although at times of me, He may try to sway.
I shall always live on the uplifting light of love;
Please send Your everlasting spirit from above.

Seek from Him

I cannot answer this question you have asked of me.
You must ask someone of far greater seed.
Ask of Him who can open your mind and let you share
All things of life you have a need for or care.
I am a man though somewhat different from you,
Yet how can I do for you what you are expected to do?
I, too, can only study and hope to understand some aspects
    of love.
You must ask the one who knows all and
Who controls the faith of our universe from above.

Giving faith and love to those who believe and call,
Sharing truth through scriptures if you but read at all.
For in every question there is that need
Of someone greater who must be of His chosen seed
To inspire us all in thoughts of prayer,
When helping other lost souls in need of care.
So trust and believe in this one spirit from above,
Knowing it is He who gives us everlasting love.

Dreams

When looking out my window toward the sky above,
I find beauty in the merger of the clouds and thoughts of
   love.
Watching clouds form pictures of all sorts of things,
For those of us who sometimes share through dreams.
Where there is beauty from contrast between gray and blue,
As in the sparkling light where it seems to shine through
That separates this solid mass,
Giving us a choice to dream in light so hard to grasp.

Like things hidden in the past, from eons ago
May often seem to drift into the light of life's afterglow,
Sharing some of the many secrets we all should hope to
   know.
That could lie ahead for those of us who long to pass,
Into the realm of time where in dreams we might find
   peace at last
When traveling into this unknown world of sublime
   fantasy,
All who care in unusual places to be,
Hop aboard my enchanting dream, let's go together and
   see.

Almost Alone

I think of days I sat in the backyard swing,
Watching and listening as my wife, Opal, would sing.
Loving her so much more for the very way
She would turn the ground in her garden and just seem
    to play.
Pulling all the weeds from around her flowers,
This could keep her outside in the garden for hours.

Then when evening came and darkness had shown,
She would leave the backyard and go into our little home,
Where we would share our loving thoughts of the day,
Being thankful to God in every way.
Maybe after supper she would watch TV or crochet
Or call one of the kids and say
That Dad had gone to the tavern to watch the Cardinals
    play.

I am quite alone now, that is to say,
Except for loving memories that often drift my way.
Yet I lose some of these thoughts when I start to pray,
As God will keep me company allowing night to display
I was almost alone yet not all the way.
Knowing You were with me, dear Lord above,
And remembering—that is the reason for all true love.

Little Girl Lost

I have not forgotten the day you chose to go away,
Just thankful you're home hopefully to stay.
I know you thought not of harm,
When crying out about some terrifying storm.
Allowing you to forget there is always the other side,
Yet for you there seemed no one in whom to confide.
Knowing you did a lot of thinking when alone,
After a few nights being unhappy, you chose to come home.

If something has been wrong and you just will not say,
Let us talk it over as a family when we once knew the way.
I know you are getting older and things seem different to
        you,
But please do not throw this life away. There are those of us
Who have always loved you and shall all life through.

Oftentimes we may speak unkindly, seeming not to
        understand
That someone is seeking or reaching for a guiding hand.
Maybe when they feel there is hope to convey problems
        within,
When talking with those that could and should care,
After you open your heart and with them truly share,
Problems you may find each day
Of things that must be talked over with someone
Who cares enough to listen and help show the way.

My Father's House

My Father's house is very close to me,
For in every little child I hope to see
All the love and truth I should give of myself free.
Of what hate could any child conceive
Other than what we choose for them to receive?
What a terrible sin some women and men must do
When they hurt a small child
Who is only seeking some love from you.

They look up to us for we are tall,
Yet some women and men are very small.
In all the hate they choose to form
Of things of the devil's charm,
They seek only the way of darkness,
Never looking for His way of light.

I pray for all souls hoping they find the way.
For what greater joy could there ever be
Than to share love with some child as lovely as she.
The one you spanked and pushed away,
Was only lonely from being hurt that day,
In need of company for a moment or two,
Then she would have left and went on to play.

Why be so selfish or sad? If you only give of yourself,
You could have all the joys of love in everything
From that loving smile a little child can bring.

Chosen Light

Is there any person who could not enjoy a smile?
Or the kindness that comes from a loving child
Sometimes saying, "I love you, Mom and Dad,
And hope to stay with you awhile"
Allowing us to be very happy never sad?
Yet some men and women hate so much;
They take out their hurt on the child they touch.
And His whole purpose in life is to give of His love,
To help us understand a special gift from above.

A being is the greatest gift there could be,
For God has chosen to instill part of His seed,
Showing us a small part of what someday we are to be.
His home is a place we may see in proper time,
Where most of us could grow to become part of His vine.
Because of knowledge we hope to always stay,
Believing it has always been this light
That helped give us faith when we chose to pray.

A Face in the Mirror

When I look at this face in the mirror,
There are many people I see.
I wonder of all there are, which of them is me?
For I am a kindly man at fault with no one,
Yet through all the smiles I might see,
There is that hate and lust within me,
Even though I erase things of harm
Seeking only to show some of my charm.

In the many people I see every day,
For them I seek happiness through prayer.
Because it is by praying for others we might share
This knowing love that is always there.
If I go out among children or men who seem to be uptight,
It is always my desire to be just in the right light
By making them feel good within my presence of sight,
When saying hello, or trying to smile and grin,
Just wishing them a nice day and a beautiful night.

These are the things I wish for in life,
So when I look into the mirror, the face I see
Will truly be of heights I hope that are within me.
Then all the faces of lust and hate,
May disappear, no longer for me to see.
I shall only see the face of God, a chosen creed,
And when this face appears my life will be free.

Memories

Poems are written about all kinds of things
About fishing holes and skating rinks.
I have a granddaughter who lives ever so near,
Who has blessed my life with thoughts very dear.
She used to play in the backyard swing,
Which was an old tire hanging from a tree,
Offering in life another sweet memory.
I built her a club house from true love shown,
So she might pretend she was playing house
With a family of hers to us unknown,
For children have dreams and fantasies of their own.

Someday she will be a wonderful wife,
In her are all the true values of life.
She is thoughtful and kind and has a loving mind
That understands the needs of others,
And I hope through prayer every now and then,
God will let her forever stay in touch with Him.
For we all live in terrible times and she may stray,
So this is why I always take the time to say,
"Always be thankful to God in every way."
Ask of Him what you may truly care to be,
For through trust and belief He will set you free.

Trust in Thee

Where should I go except onward unto Thee,
The One who has chosen to have called me
To share a joy from spreading Your way of light,
Through my poems that shall be written
Only with Thee in sight.

Knowing we can only push truth away so long,
Then it starts haunting us a lonely song
That seems to say something of Your word
About all the truths I know of life,
Yet most have never even heard.
There is evil in life on earth that we all have shared,
Until most of us could no longer seem to bear.

So if you are a person somewhat like me,
Open your mind where truth and peace can dwell.
Believe by loving all people, giving of yourself,
You will help in this story all must tell.

Gift of Sight

Open your heart and mind as well;
Let all the good things of life forever dwell.
Like the sun and stars, also the moon above,
But the greatest gift of all is your true love.

Sharing moments through peace of brotherhood,
Allowing this great strength to show its good.
Think each day of others or what they often do,
Showing you care for them in your daily prayer, too.
Just open your eyes and learn to see
That all good things on earth are here for you and me.

Really take the time and try to say hello;
Smile once in a while and truly let yourself go.
For all of the love that is resting inside
Is just bursting to come alive.
I have said it before and I shall say it again:
Open your heart and just throw your love into the wind.
By doing so,
Perhaps somewhere in life you will find another friend.

The Upper Berth

When you think of heaven or where it might be,
Do you open your heart and mind to truly see
That these truths are within you and me?
They are here and there and almost anywhere,
Just longing to show some comfort or need,
From the many blessings of God within sent free.

All that He may ask yet some feel is a command
Is that we think of each other as the brother of man.
Living in sight of His laws that were chosen right
For all of us who should be longing for this light
That will show the way through happiness, if we care
When just asking of Him in prayer
That overflowing love to share.

So when you start looking for your heaven or upper berth,
Remember the Bible does say it will be on God's new earth.
Please do not get in a hurry to leave, trust and believe,
These laws have been written to set man free.
The commandments you should read and try to
        understand,
Are a special gift that have been chosen for man.

Try to develop your mind and body as well,
Being humble when seeking the way of truth that is to tell.
When the last horn blows and this old earth's time has been,
There shall be a place of contentment from the life within.

Free

I would like to tell the world
Of the many joys I choose to share,
When being with You Lord, one who will always care,
Who lets me walk in the many truths I find each day,
Knowing when I wake in each morning I could say
We took the time together to start me on my way.
Also, you let me see all the beauty that is everywhere,
For those of us who should care to share.

Yet like most we forget too easily,
Sometimes only thinking of lust, hate, or greed.
We believe we should receive everything very fast,
As if this old world isn't going to last.
Though You and I know better,
Because You shall comfort those who trust and believe.
When changing their ways, most problems and tribulations
Never need be.
For in trust of Your light we can all learn to see,
No greater joy could ever be than truth that sets one free.

Opal, My Love

Opal is my love like the stars above
To light up my life forever after.
I think of the time she chose to be mine,
Always with true love and laughter.
When dancing together in one place or another,
We felt this special glow
Would shine for all time as no other.
Believing our love was forever to be in access
For I had really been blessed in thoughts
That never seem to rest
When longing and caring about her.

Soon time may come and we, as all, must part,
Yet Opal, my love, you will always share my heart.
For love that's true will always endure
And share shall we forever
In that one great moment in afterlife to be,
Believing our faith shall always allow lovers
To bloom again those that think as you and me.

Solitude

Some may think I am a lonely man
In my many hours of solitude.
They do not seem to understand
For they know not of you,
The one who lets me share living again.
A way of life,
With peace of mind, not strife.
It's not the life we once knew,
Yet for me this solitude will do.

For what is life other than living each and every day?
May we find that rest to remind us
Of this unjust price we could pay.

Yet the lucky ones that are kept together
Surely will try to make the run,
For in life they have just begun.
What glory is there beyond the sun
Greater than two becoming one?

Someone

At times my room seems quite lonely
Yet you're never far away,
No further than a thought of yesterday,
Where we could relive again a life we once knew,
Of joy and happiness we chose to share
Because of faith and taking time to care.

So when my days seem dreary,
I somehow really don't care,
I remember the wants and loves of life
That we both shared.
Like swimming together or dancing to a lovely song,
Sadness comes and goes but happy memories linger on.

For our life was a happy one although all people
Could not care,
Yet if they would ask of me with them I would share
All the beautiful moments of love and joy,
Where people truly think of others and believe
They are also in need,
Remembering the truths of our Lord and His seed.
To enlighten the spirit of all life we see,
Allowing us moments through His love
When bringing us together forever to be free.

When Growing Old

When growing old so few people seem to understand
They're playing a part on this earth, which is a stage.
We are its actors of different colors, body shapes, and age.
We start as babies who need help from someone greater.
This never stops our whole life through,
For we all need someone to guide and help us no matter
What we ever chose to do.

Yet as time goes on when families grow and depart,
We will lose that part of love and closeness we shared
Because of our change of address and not being there,
We now find ourselves out on some stage quite alone,
Like old people somehow playing a game,
Some misguided with feelings of a terrible shame.
We color our hair, that is, what is left of it; use too much
Makeup or perfume just to try to stay in touch.
Yet our services are somehow like us getting old,
Though I sometimes resent
When others think I always have to be told.

Yet I never quite looked at life this way,
For I chose to be as one who would learn to see
By living in the Master's way who judges all life to be.
Having me perform in different stages of man,
From birth through childhood, to be a man and understand
So I may learn through growing older to share of His
    Command.

There's a reason for being on this stage that has been set
    from above.
For I read scripture that tells of a plan,
Whereby loving and believing in Him.
I, too, will know of life that ever was or ever will be again.
Knowing in the game of life I might always see,
People all around me are more than just lost souls,
For within my heart they shall always be brothers and
Sisters to forever share my cup of tea.

So never be sad when growing old, just be glad you chose
    to play.
Knowing you still treasure many thoughts within your
    mind,
Not only of life from yesterday, but of life today in time.
Look around and you will see a lot of older friends
Who are looking toward this life as thee.
Where in this day of doubt as age becomes to some a misery,
I can see you're just as I am, truly thanking God for His plan
Allowing you and I to remain a member of the family of
    man.

Such a Wonder

Life is such a wonder by His each and every commandment,
You need but live within His love to understand
That all things are free through love and trust in time.
For the happiness you're apt to seek is as open as His door,
Yet it is you who must knock and honor and adore.
Always believing you will have the chance to dine,
Gained through prayer with loving moments He makes
    sublime.
Allowing His words taught through scripture since given
    time,
Telling us to go forward in a special way,
Remembering the coming of the end and its sign.

Sharing in this strength of light through love each day,
Although some chose to forget or say its strange to pray.
Yet who are they? No more than men made of clay
Who live each day somehow without worry or strife,
Not thinking prayer makes any difference in life.
Though I have found in given time,
Man often reaps what he is apt to sow,
Leaving him to better himself of mind
When reading scripture, which will enlighten his soul.

River's Edge

I sit on the bank of a mighty river
At the locks at Alton town.
My thoughts often take me there
Whenever I feel depressed or let down.
Most of my thinking occurs
When no one is around.
I find sitting on the river's edge brings thoughts
Of you alone;
Memories shared of happy times to others unknown.

Although death became my enemy,
I will never give up in what's to be,
Allowing me to share in dreams at river's edge,
A place that brings you close to me.
Yet I know that when my dreams are over
And once more when I must face life that is real,
I will have the truth in life
To put on a more encouraging keel.

Just like the water gushing
Through the locks at Alton town,
I, too, must head toward river's end,
Leaving all these thoughts and dreams to
Settle down.
For of each day's light I truly know,
I shall be given that chance once more to grow,
To sit again on river's edge and watch the water flow
Into that certain place below each bend
Where all things that have been lost come together again.